TECH TALK

HOW THE INTERNET WORKS

by Martha London

Consultant: Beth Gambro
Reading Specialist, Yorkville, Illinois

BEARPORT PUBLISHING

Bearcub Books, an imprint of Bearport Publishing by FlutterBee

Teaching Tips

Before Reading

- Look at the cover of the book. Discuss the picture and the title.
- Ask readers to brainstorm a list of what they already know about the internet. What can they expect to see in the book?
- Go on a picture walk, looking through the pictures to discuss vocabulary and make predictions about the text.

During Reading

- Read for purpose. Encourage readers to think about how the internet works as they are reading.
- Ask readers to look for the details of the book. What are some ways they use this kind of technology in their own lives?
- If readers encounter an unknown word, ask them to look at the sounds in the word. Then, ask them to look at the rest of the page. Are there any clues to help them understand?

After Reading

- Encourage readers to pick a buddy and reread the book together.
- Ask readers to name two things that happen for your computer to get info from the internet. Find the pages that tell about these things.
- Ask readers to write or draw something they learned about the internet.

Credits
Cover and title page, © BGStock72/Adobe Stock and © dashu83/Adobe Stock and © Alena/Adobe Stock; 3, © Macrovector/Adobe Stock; 5, © wavebreak3/Adobe Stock; 7, © True Images/Alamy Stock Photo; 9, © Gorodenkoff/Adobe Stock; 11, © BrianAJackson/iStock; 12, © Miquel/Adobe Stock; 13, © David Fleetham/Alamy Stock Photo; 14-15, © Olga Yastremska/Adobe Stock; 17, © FangXiaNuo/iStock; 19, © evgenyatamanenko/iStock; 21, © Seventyfour/Adobe Stock; 22TR, © Allan Cash Picture Library/Alamy Stock Photo; 22ML, © Gorodenkoff/Adobe Stock; 22BR, © pikselstock/Adobe Stock; 23TL, © BillionPhotos/Adobe Stock; 23TM, © sdecoret/Adobe Stock; 23TR, © Maren Winter/Adobe Stock; 23BL, © phaitoon/Adobe Stock; 23BM, © Olga Yastremska/Adobe Stock; 23BR, © vectorfusionart/Adobe Stock

See BearportPublishing.com for our statement on Generative AI Usage.

Library of Congress Cataloging-in-Publication Data is available at www.loc.gov or upon request from the publisher.

ISBN: 979-8-89577-578-3 (hardcover)
ISBN: 979-8-89577-758-9 (paperback)
ISBN: 979-8-89577-666-7 (ebook)

For more information, write to Bearport Publishing, 3500 American Blvd W, Suite 150, Bloomington, MN 55431.
Printed in the United States of America.

Contents

Go Online!

Do you have a question?

You can find answers on the internet.

But how does the internet work?

The internet is a **network** of computers and **devices**.

It connects tech all around the world.

This lets people everywhere share info.

youtube.com
jack54hd
Up next
Upload
Sign in
FEEL THE GAME
117,815
SQUAD BUILDER SHOWDOWN W/ AJ3FIFA AND PINK CAVANI!! - FIFA 15 ULTIMATE TEAM
Subscribe

Some computers hold lots of info.

These are called **servers**.

They send info to other tech around the world.

How does your computer get this info?

First, your computer has to ask for it.

It sends a message through the network.

Search or type a URL

This message often moves through **cables**.

Many internet cables are underground.

Some are even under the sea!

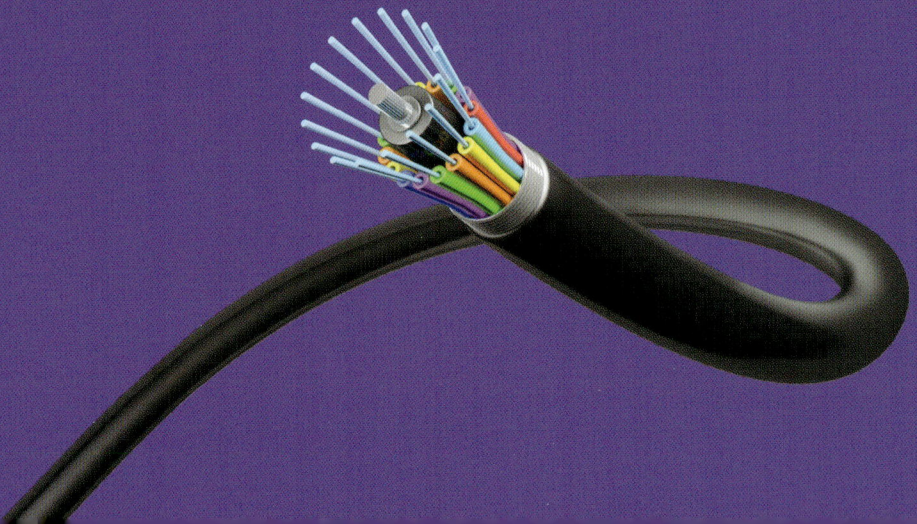

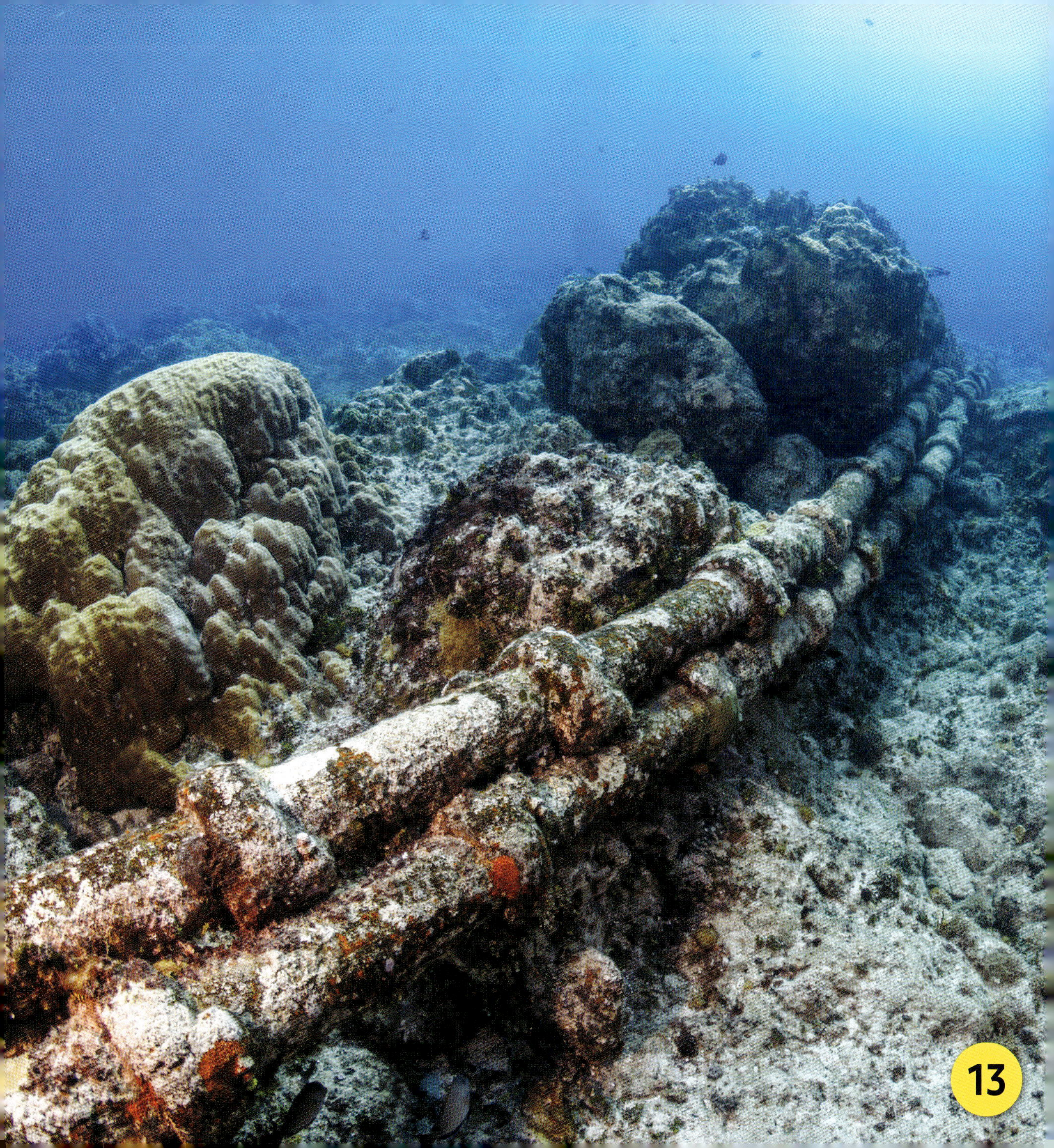

Info can also move through the air using Wi-Fi.

Your computer turns it into radio waves.

These waves go to a **router**.

A router

The router and cables get the message to a server.

The server sends info back.

It travels to your computer.

No matter how the message travels, the internet is fast.

All kinds of info can get to you in seconds.

Wow!

The internet is important in many parts of our lives.

People use it to work.

They also use it for fun.

How do you use the internet?

The Internet Over Time

The early internet connected only a few computers.

Over time, more people were connected to the internet. But it was very slow.

Now, the internet is very fast. It has a lot of info to explore.

Glossary

cables strong wires made of steel or fiber

devices machines such as smartwatches, smartphones, and tablets

network a group of parts joined together

radio waves invisible waves sent through the air to make many devices work

router a device that moves info within a computer network

servers computers that store and send information

Index

Read More

Gifford, Clive. *Learning Online (Computer Kids).* New York: Rosen Publishing, 2026.

Peters, Katie. *Being Safe Online: A First Look (Read About Citizenship).* Minneapolis: Lerner Publications, 2024.

Learn More Online

1. Go to **FactSurfer.com** or scan the QR code below.
2. Enter "**How Internet Works**" into the search box.
3. Click on the cover of this book to see a list of websites.

About the Author

Martha London lives and works in Minnesota. She has two cats and loves to go on hikes outside.